Share Time

HOUGHTON MIFFLIN HARCOURT
School Publishers

Photo credits

Cover © George Doyle/Getty Images. **Title** Stockbyte/Getty Images. **19** © Philip Mugridge/Alamy. **20** © Tracy Hebden/Alamy. **21** © Peter Arnold, Inc./Alamy. **22** © Corbis. **23** © Gary Salter/zefa/Corbis. **24** © Eric and David Hosking/Corbis. **43** © Martin Harvey/Corbis. **44** © Corbis Premium RF/Alamy. **45** © Chris Newbert/Minden Pictures. **46** © KAMARULZAMAN RUSSALI/Reuters/Corbis. **47** © Frans Lanting/Minden Pictures. **48** © George H. H. Huey/Corbis. **49** © B.A.E. Inc./Alamy. **50** © Wim Wiskerke/Alamy. **51** © JUPITERIMAGES/Thinkstock/Alamy. **52** © Jill Stephenson/Alamy. **53** © JUPITERIMAGES/Creatas/Alamy. **54** © JUPITERIMAGES/BananaStock/Alamy. **73** Brand X Pictures. **74** © 1998 EyeWire, Inc./Getty Images. **75** © Blend Images/Alamy. **76** © Vario Images GmbH & Co.KG/Alamy. **77** Blend Images/SuperStock. **78** Stockbyte/Getty Images. **97** © Mike Harrington/Alamy. **98** © i love images/Alamy. **99** © PhotoAlto/Alamy. **100** © Clare Charleson/Alamy. (inset, tennis ball) Artville. **101** © Nick Hanna/Alamy. **102** © AM Corporation/Alamy. All other photo's are the property of Houghton Mifflin Harcourt.

Contents

Phonics

Words with Double Consonants and <u>ck</u> Read each sentence. Tell which picture it goes with. Then point to and read each name.

Jack will pack a sack.

Zack will pack hats.

Max will pack socks.

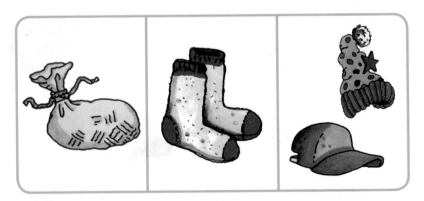

Ann Packs

by Ellen Catala

illustrated by Diane Paterson

"I miss Ann. I can call Ann.
Ann can come here," said Nan.

"Yes," said Ann. "I will come.
I will be quick, Nan."

Quick, quick, quick!
Ann will pack a big red bag.

Ann will pack ten hats.
Ann will pack ten socks.
Pack, pack, pack, pack.

Ann will pack six ducks.
Ann will pack ten dolls.
Pack, pack, pack, pack.

Ann has hats and socks.

Ann has ducks and dolls.

Ann has ten big hugs for Nan.

TEKS 1.1B identify upper- and lower-case letters; **1.21B(ii)** capitalize pronoun "I"

Capitalization (Read Together)

Pronoun I When **I** is a word, it is written with a capital letter. Read these sentences.

Can I call Ann?
Ann said, "I will come."
I will pack six hats.

Find the letter **i**. When is it a lower-case letter? When is it a capital letter? Write a sentence about yourself using **I**.

9

Phonics

Words with Double Consonants and <u>ck</u> Read the words to go up and down the hill. Use two or more of the words in a sentence.

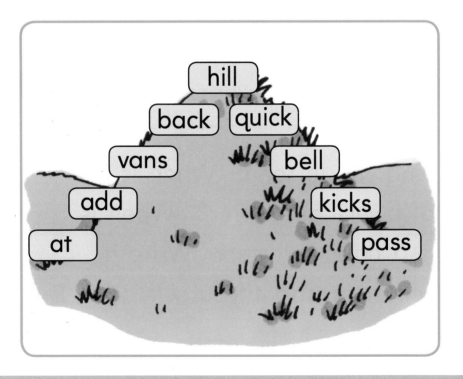

Tess and Jack

by Timothy Bern

illustrated by Marsha Winborn

"Call me," said Tess.

"Call me," said Jack.

11

Tess is sick. Tess is sick in bed.
Tess cannot play, but Tess can
call Jack.

Jack is sick. Jack is sick in bed.
Jack cannot play, but Jack can
call Tess.

Tess is well. Tess is back. Tess
can play. Jack is well. Jack is
back. Jack can play. Tess and
Jack can bat.

"I will get a mitt," said Tess.

"I will get a bat," said Jack.

"Hit it, Jack," said Tess. "Quick!
Hit it. Get a run."

Will Jack call Tess?
Yes! Yes! Jack will.
Will Tess call Jack?
Yes! Yes! Tess will.

16

TEKS 1.5 read aloud with fluency/comprehension; **1.21B(ii)** capitalize pronoun "I"; **ELPS 1A** use prior knowledge/experiences

Fluency

Expression Read "Tess and Jack" aloud with a partner. Take turns on each page. Use your feelings to help you read with expression.

Pronoun I Find the letter **i** in the story. When is it a capital letter? Tell why.

Phonics

Words with Double Consonants and <u>ck</u>

Read all the words. Find three words with <u>ck</u> in a row. Read those words again.

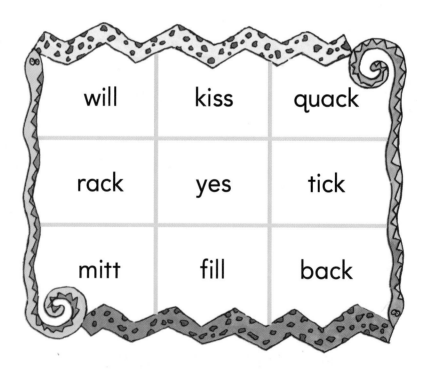

will	kiss	quack
rack	yes	tick
mitt	fill	back

Ducks Quack

by Kyle Stenovich

Look up at the ducks.
Quack, quack, quack.
Hear the ducks quack.

Look at the ducks.

Ducks can see rocks and mud.

Ducks will nip. Ducks will peck.

Ducks will go in.

Ducks will get wet.

Ducks will quack.

Quack, quack, quack.

Look at the ducks.

Ducks will dip in.

Dip, dip, dip.

Ducks will pop back up.
Pop, pop, pop.

Hear the duck on the hill.
Every duck can quack.
Quack, quack, quack.

TEKS 1.23A generate topics/ formulate questions; **1.23B** determine relevant sources of information
ELPS 3E share information in cooperative learning interactions

Research

Read Together

Share What You Know

Discuss with a partner what you know about ducks.

Questions What would you like to learn about ducks? With your partner, write some questions you have about ducks. Tell how you could find answers to these questions.

Phonics

Words with Consonant Clusters with r Read the words. What is the second letter in each word? Read the words again. Listen for the sound for r.

Brad and Cris

by Teresa Bashin

illustrated by Marsha Winborn

Brad Frog is red. Brad has tan
dots. Brad is red and tan.

Brad has a pal. His pal is Cris.
Cris Frog is tan. Cris has no
dots. Cris is tan and red.

"We will go on a trip, Cris,"
Brad said. "It will be fun."
Brad did not tell Cris why.

Brad led Cris. Brad and Cris
hop on pads. Hop, hop! Hop,
hop, hop!

"Can we get some bugs and
grubs?" said Cris.
"Not yet," said Brad. "Not yet."

"Look, Brad!" Cris said. "Bugs, bugs, bugs! Grubs, grubs, grubs! Yum!"

Book Information

Book Parts Point to the parts of a book.

The **title** is the name of the story. The **author** is the person who wrote the story. The **illustrator** is the person who drew the pictures.

TEKS **1.3A** decode words in context and in isolation; **1.3C(i)** decode using closed syllables; **1.3E** read words with inflectional endings

Phonics

Words with Consonant Clusters with <u>r</u>

Read the words in the box. Read the sentences. Use the words to complete the sentences.

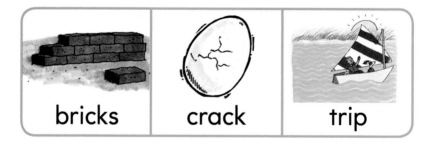

| bricks | crack | trip |

1. Gram and Fran go on a ____.

2. Brad fills his truck with ____.

3. The eggs drop and ____!

What Did Dad Get?

by Ed Floyd

illustrated by Julia Gorton

Fred has a big bag. Gram has a
tan cap. It is for Dad.

Fred can hold up the bag. Gram
will drop the tan cap in it. Pop!

Jill can get the bag. Jill has an
animal. It is a red frog!

Pop! Jill drops the red frog in the
bag. It is for Dad.

"Gram," said Fred, "Dad has a
red frog. How did Dad get it?"

Dad has his tan cap. Dad has a
red frog on top of his cap. Fred,
Jill, and Gram grin at Dad.

TEKS **1.17A** generate ideas for writing; **1.17E** publish/share writing; **1.18A** write brief stories

Writing

Plan Think about a gift you have given someone. Draw a picture of it. Then discuss it with a partner.

Write and Share Write a short story with your partner about giving gifts. Share it with the class.

Phonics

Words with Consonant Clusters with r Read the first word. Say the words that name the pictures. Tell which word rhymes with the first word. Write the two rhyming words on paper.

The Big Job

by Pamela Chin

illustrated by John Ceballos

Dad has a job. Dad will go to his
job. Sid has a job. Sid will go to
his job.

Dad has a big red truck.
Dad will lug bricks in his truck.

Sid has a red truck. Sid will drop
his bricks on the grass.

Dad will dig up lots of rocks.
Dig, dig, dig, Dad!

Sid will dig up lots of rocks.
Dig, dig, dig, Sid!

Dad is back with Sid.
Why will Sid sit with Dad?
Dad and Sid will play!

Use Strategies

Read Together

Read for Understanding Reread **The Big Job** on pages 43–48 carefully.

Correct and Adjust As you read the story, you might not understand a part of it. Do one or more of these things to help you:

- Reread it aloud.
- Picture in your mind what it is about.
- Think about what you already know about jobs people do using trucks.
- Ask yourself a question about the meaning, such as **What does Dad do with the bricks?**

TEKS **1.3A** decode words in isolation; **1.3C(i)** decode using closed syllables; **1.3D** decode words with common spelling patterns

Phonics

Words with Consonant Clusters with l Read the words on the flags. Use two or more words in a sentence.

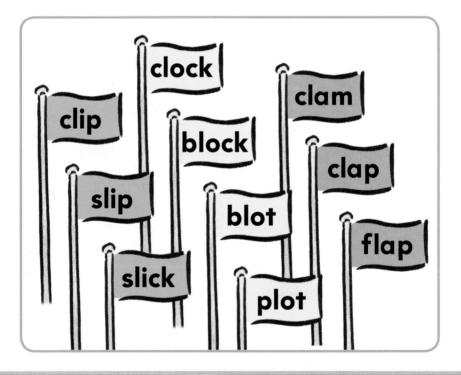

Our Flag
by Susan Crowton

Up, up, up. The flag is on top.
It can flap. It can flip.

Up, up, up. The flag is on top.
It can flip. It can flap.

Our club has a big flag. We will
sing. We will clap.

The flag is big. It is flat. They
hold it up, up, up. They will not
let it drop.

Flags can flip. Flags can flap.
Kids hold flags up, up, up.
Flags flap. Flags flip.

Flags, flags, flags. Pam has a flag. She is glad she has it.

TEKS 1.26 create visual display/dramatization **ELPS 1C** use strategic learning techniques to acquire vocabulary

Connections (Read Together)

Make a Flag Think of what you learned about flags from the story "Our Flag." Think about flags you have seen.

Draw your own flag. Tell a partner why you like your flag. Where would you like to fly your flag?

1.3A decode words in isolation; **1.3C(i)** decode using closed syllables; **1.3D** decode words with common spelling patterns

Phonics

Words with Consonant Clusters with l These words are mixed up. Read the words. Write all the words with short <u>o</u> in one list. Write words with other vowels in another list. Read each list.

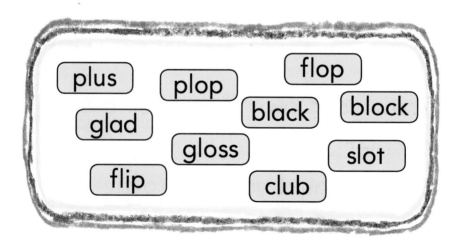

The Plan

by Martin Avalong
illustrated by Linda Bronson

Hen has a plan. Cluck, cluck,
cluck. Hen will tell it to Duck.
Run, Hen! Run, run!

Did Duck like her plan? Yes, yes,
yes! Duck flaps, flaps, flaps. Duck
claps, claps, claps. Hen and Duck
will play today.

Duck and Hen will have fun. Hen
trips, slips, and flips. Duck will,
too. Trip, trip, trip! Slip, slip, slip!
Flip, flip, flip!

Hen claps, flaps, and slaps. Duck will, too. Clap, flap, slap!

Hen flops, clops, and plops. Duck
will, too. Flop, clop, plop!

Hen quits. Duck quits. Hen had a
good plan. Now it is good to sit.
Sit, sit, sit!

Decoding Read Together

Read Carefully   Read this
story.

A bug nips. Hen flaps.
The bug flips and
zips and nips.

Hen slaps.
The bug quits and Hen flops.

Think   Do you think you read
every word correctly? If a word
is hard to read, how can you
figure it out? Reread the story.

Phonics

Words with Consonant Clusters with l Read the sentences. Match the sentences with the pictures. Then point to and read words with clusters with l.

Fluff is a big black dog.

Does Glenn like to cluck?

Slim is a cat with a plan.

The Pet Club

by Ellen Catala
illustrated by Molly Delaney

Would you like to see pets?
Come to The Pet Club.

Dom has a pet. His pet is Ham.
Ham can flip. Ham can flop.

Roz has a pet cat. Her pet is
Glenn. Glenn can kick.

Todd has a pet dog. His pet is
Slim. Slim can run. Slim can sit.

Ann has a pet. Her pet is Bluff.
Bluff can clack. Bluff can flap.

Nick has a pet. His pet is Plum.
Plum will not flip, flop, and clack.
Plum will not play, but Plum will kiss!

Vocabulary

Read Together

Action Words

flip   kick   run   sip   kiss

Act It Out   Work with a partner. Read the words. Then write each word on a card. Choose a card. Act out the word. See if your partner can guess the word from your actions. Then have your partner act out a word and you try to guess the action.

Phonics

Words with Consonant Clusters with s Read each question. Find the picture that answers it. Then point to and read words that begin with a cluster with s.

What did Stan set up?

What did Skip pet?

What did Kim step on?

Step Up!

by Tanya Rivers

The clock struck 8.
We go to the bus stop.
Step up! Step up!

Can Jess read?   Yes, Jess can!
Can Stan read?   Yes, Stan can!

Kim can write A, B, C.
Kim can spell.

Jill will snap blocks.

Jill will snap stacks and stacks.

We pick a good spot.

Peg will spin. Bess will spin.

Jen will spin.

Is it fun to step, step, step?
Is it fun to skip and sing?
Yes, it is! It is fun, fun, fun!

TEKS 1.4B ask questions/seek clarification/locate details about texts; **1.4C** establish purpose/monitor comprehension **ELPS** 2I demonstrate listening comprehension of spoken English

Use Strategies

Read Together

Ask Questions To help you understand a story better, ask yourself questions as you read. Then read on to find the answers.

Read **Step Up!** on pages 75–80 again. If you do not understand a part or want to know more, ask yourself questions about the story. Then read the words and look at the pictures to find the answers.

TEKS 1.3A decode words in context and in isolation; **1.3C(i)** decode using closed syllables; **1.3E** decode words with inflectional endings

Phonics

Words with Consonant Clusters with s Read each sentence and find the matching picture. Then reread words that begin with a cluster with s.

Meg draws red spots.

Stan sleds on the hill.

Rex steps up.

Splat! Splat!

by Svetlana Yarmey
illustrated by Rusty Fletcher

Meg has on a red smock.
Stan has on a tan smock.

83

Splat! Splat! Meg will draw
spots. Meg will draw dots.
What good pictures Meg has!

Snip! Snap! Stan will snip scraps.
Stan will snap blocks. What good
trucks Stan has!

Yum! Yum! Mom has snacks.
Stan will stop for a snack. Stan
has a big snack.

Stan has his snack. Yum! Yum!
Will Meg stop for a snack? Will
Meg skip her snack?

Meg will skip it.
Splat! Splat! Splat!

TEKS 1.3A(iii) decode words with consonant blends; **1.6A** identify nouns/verbs; **1.6D** categorize words; **ELPS 1C** use strategic learning techniques to acquire vocabulary

Words

Verbs and Nouns   Read these words.

> draw scraps smock snip trucks

Draw a chart like this one:

Actions	Things

Use the chart to sort the words from the box that name actions and words that name things. Add more words.

TEKS **1.3A** decode words in isolation; **1.3D** decode words with common spelling patterns; **1.3E** decode words with inflectional endings

Phonics

Words with Consonant Clusters with s Read the words on each ladder. Tell which words rhyme. Tell what sounds are the same in the rhyming words.

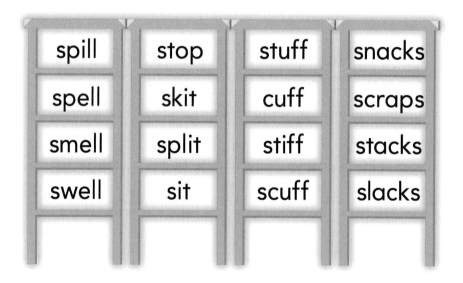

spill	stop	stuff	snacks
spell	skit	cuff	scraps
smell	split	stiff	stacks
swell	sit	scuff	slacks

Miss Tess Was Still

by Ted Lutgen

illustrated by Mircea Catusanu

Miss Tess was still. Miss Tess was
as still as a stick.

Now Miss Tess will skip.
Skip! Skip! Skip!

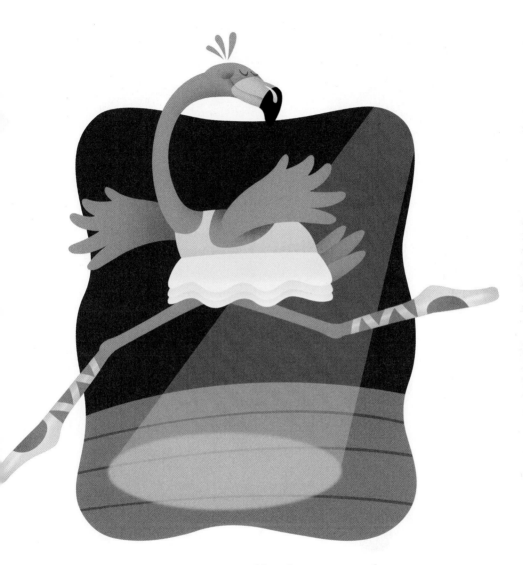

Miss Tess will do a split.
Split! Split! Split!

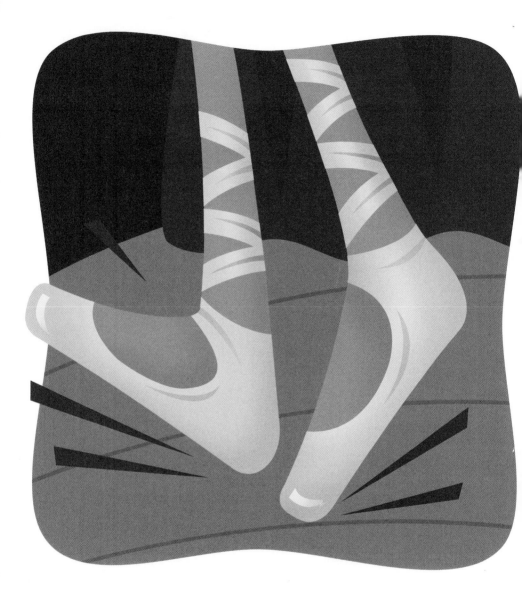

Miss Tess will step and tap.
Step! Step! Tap! Tap! Tap!

Miss Tess will spin. Miss Tess will spin like a top. Spin! Spin! Spin!

Miss Tess has to stop. Miss Tess
will be still. Miss Tess will grin.
Click! Click! Click!

TEKS **1.17B** develop drafts; **1.20A(i)** understand/use verbs; **1.21B(ii)** capitalize pronoun "I"; **ELPS** **5B** write using new basic/content-based vocabulary

Writing

Plan and Write Read these words.

skip   split   step   tap   spin

Draw a picture of a way you like to move. Write a sentence that goes with your picture. Use a verb from the box.

Remember Capitalize the word *I*.

Phonics

Words with Final Consonant Clusters   Read the words on the shells.   Tell which words end with consonant clusters.

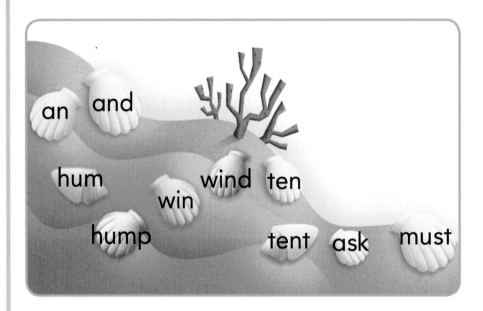

an   and

hum   wind   ten

win

hump   tent   ask   must

Who Likes to Jump?

by Cyrus Rivera

It is fun to jump. Gus and Liz
went to play. Gus and Liz run
and jump on a sand hill.

Fran will hop, jump, and land
on 7. Next, Fran will hop, jump
and land on 8 and 9.

Jill will grasp the ends with her hands. Jill will jump as fast as she can. Jump, jump, jump!

Russ must jump and hit. Russ can jump up, up, up. Russ can hit. Russ can jump and hit.

Len is on a track. Len will run like
the wind. Len will bend his legs
and jump, jump, jump.

It is fun to take small jumps and big jumps. Jump, jump, jump!

Letters

Identify Names

Jill   hill   jump   Gus   hit

1. Point to and read two names. What kind of letter do they begin with?

2. Point to and read the word that ends with a **t**. Is it a name? How do you know?

3. Which words are not names? How do you know?

TEKS **1.3A** decode words in context and in isolation; **1.3C(i)** decode using closed syllables;
1.3E decode words with inflectional endings

Phonics

Words with Final Consonant Clusters Read each sentence. Tell which picture it goes with. Point to and read the words that end with consonant clusters.

> **Russ must rest.**
> **Trent can jump in mud.**
> **Grant will hunt for a nut.**

The Lost Cat

by Jane Nicholas

illustrated by Kristen Goeters

"Mick!" said Bess. "Muff is lost!
Ask Trent to help us."

Trent is at his desk.

"Muff is lost? Yes! Yes! I will help," said Trent. "We must find Muff!"

Trent plans his task.

"Hunt," Trent said. "We must hunt and hunt and hunt."

"Here is one hint. Cat tracks!
Tracks can take us to Muff."

Trent went past the plant stand.
At last, Trent can see Muff.

Muff is not lost! Muff has small
kits. Muff and her kits will rest
and rest.

Retelling

Events Think about these things from "The Lost Cat."

1. Trent's desk Name Jass copy
2. the plant stand
3. Muff and her kits
   Her

Draw Make a map that shows these things. Draw cat tracks to show where Bess and Mick went. Use your map to retell the story to a partner.

113

Phonics

Words with Final Consonant Clusters Name the pictures. Read the words. Name the pictures and words that rhyme. Use two rhyming words in a sentence.

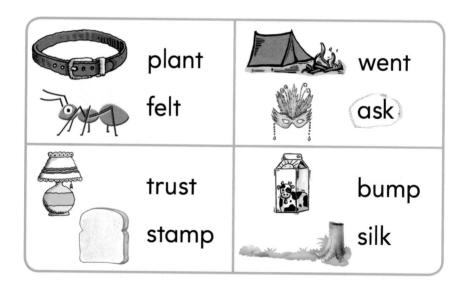

plant
felt

went
ask

trust
stamp

bump
silk

The List

by Ellen Catala

illustrated by Dorothy Donahue

"Take this list," Mom tells Brent.
"Run and get what is on the list."

Brent runs fast. Brent runs
too fast! He drops his list.

Brent is at the stand. Brent hunts
and hunts, but his list is lost.

Brent gets stamps, eggs, and
buns. Brent gets nuts and mints.

Brent put the sack on his back.
Brent did not stop to eat a snack.

"I lost the list," Brent tells Mom,
"but I got stamps, eggs, buns,
nuts, and mints."
"Brent is the best!" said Mom.

Use Strategies

Ask Questions To help you understand a story better, ask yourself questions as you read. Then read carefully to find the answers.

Read **The List** on pages 115–120 again. If you do not understand a part or want to know more, ask yourself questions, such as: **Why does Brent hunt for the list on page 117? Does Brent buy the right things?** Then read the words and look at the pictures to find the answers.

Phonics

Read to Review   Use what you know about sounds and letters to read the words.

Words with <u>ck</u>

| back | rock | luck | neck |
| clock | snack | quick | quack |

Double Consonants

| add | doll | bell | mitt |
| glass | grill | floss | spell |

Final Consonant Clusters

| ask | last | left | pond |
| send | best | stump | crust |

Consonant Clusters with <u>r</u>, <u>l</u>, and <u>s</u>

trick	trap	dress	drop
crack	brick	press	print
black	glad	clock	class
flag	glass	plum	plant
stop	stamp	sled	spell
slip	snack	sniff	spend

Build and Read Words   Put the letters together to read the words. Think of more words to add.

k ick

p ick

b r ick

b and

h and

s t and

b ump

j ump

s t ump

123

Word Lists

Accompanies
"Jack and the Wolf"

Ann Packs
page 2

Decodable Words
Target Skill: Short *a*
Ann, bag, can, has, hats, Nan, pack, packs

Target Skills: Double Final Consonants and *ck*
Ann, dolls, ducks, miss, pack, packs, quick, socks, will

Previously Taught Skills
big, hugs, red, six, ten, yes

High-Frequency Words
New
call, come, said

Previously Taught
a, and, be, for, here, I

Tess and Jack
page 10

Decodable Words
Target Skill: Short *a*
back, bat, can, cannot, Jack

Target Skills: Double Final Consonants and *ck*
back, Jack, mitt, quick, sick, Tess, well, will

Previously Taught Skills
bed, but, get, hit, in, is, it, run, yes

High-Frequency Words
New
call, said

Previously Taught
a, and, I, me, play

Ducks Quack

Decodable Words

Target Skill: Short *a*
at, back, can, quack

Target Skills: Double Final Consonants and *ck*
back, duck, ducks, hill, peck, quack, rocks, will

Previously Taught Skills
dip, get, in, mud, nip, on, pop, up, wet

High-Frequency Words

New
every, hear

Previously Taught
and, go, look, see, the

Brad and Cris

page 26

Decodable Words
Target Skill: Short *i*
Cris, did, his, is, it, trip, will

Target Skill: Clusters with *r*
Brad, Cris, Frog, grubs, trip

Previously Taught Skills
bugs, can, dots, fun, get, has, hop, led, not, on, pads, pal, red, tan, tell, yet, yum

High-Frequency Words
New
some, why

Previously Taught
a, and, go, look, no, said, we

What Did Dad Get?

page 34

Decodable Words
Target Skill: Short *i*
big, did, grin, his, in, is, it, Jill, will

Target Skill: Clusters with *r*
drop, drops, Fred, frog, Gram, grin

Previously Taught Skills
an, at, bag, can, cap, Dad, get, has, on, pop, red, tan, top, up

High-Frequency Words
New
animal, how, of

Previously Taught
a, and, for, hold, said, the, what

The Big Job

page 42

Decodable Words

Target Skill: Short *i*
big, bricks, dig, his, in, is, Sid, sit, will

Target Skill: Clusters with *r*
bricks, drop, grass, truck

Previously Taught Skills
back, Dad, has, job, lots, lug, red, rocks, on, up

High-Frequency Words

New
of, why

Previously Taught
a, and, go, play, the, to, with

Our Flag

page 50

Decodable Words
Target Skill: Short *o*
drop, not, on, top

Target Skill: Clusters with *l*
clap, club, flag, flags, flap, flat, flip, glad

Previously Taught Skills
big, can, has, is, it, kids, let, Pam, up, will

High-Frequency Words
New
our, she

Previously Taught
hold, sing, the, they, we

The Plan

page 58

Decodable Words
Target Skill: Short *o*
clop, clops, flop, flops, plop, plops

Target Skill: Clusters with *l*
clap, claps, clop, clops, cluck, flap, flaps,
flip, flips, flop, flops, plan, plop, plops,
slap, slaps, slip, slips

Previously Taught Skills
but, did, Duck, fun, had, has, Hen, is, it,
quits, run, sit, tell, trip, trips, will, yes

High-Frequency Words
New
her, today

Previously Taught
a, and, good, have, like,
play, the, to, too

The Pet Club

page 66

Decodable Words

Target Skill: Short *o*
dog, Dom, flop, not, Roz, Todd

Target Skill: Clusters with *l*
Bluff, clack, club, flap, flip, flop, Glenn, Plum, Slim

Previously Taught Skills
Ann, but, can, cat, Ham, has, his, is, kick, kiss, Nick, pet, pets, run, sit, will

High-Frequency Words

New
her, would

Previously Taught
a, and, come, like, see, the, to, you

Accompanies
"Meet Dr. Seuss"

Step Up!

page 74

Decodable Words
Target Skill: Short *e*
Bess, Jen, Jess, Peg, spell, step, yes

Target Skill: Clusters with *s*
skip, snap, spell, spin, spot, stacks,
Stan, step, stop, struck

Previously Taught Skills
8, A, B, C, blocks, bus, can, clock, fun,
is, it, Jill, Kim, pick, up, will

High-Frequency Words
New
read, write

Previously Taught
a, and, go, good, sing, the,
to, we

Splat! Splat!

page 82

Decodable Words
Target Skill: Short *e*
Meg, red

Target Skill: Clusters with *s*
scraps, skip, smock, snack, snacks,
snap, snip, splat, spots, Stan, stop

Previously Taught Skills
big, blocks, dots, has, his, it, Mom, on,
tan, trucks, will, yum

High-Frequency Words
New
draw, pictures

Previously Taught
a, for, good, have, her, what

130

Miss Tess Was Still

page 90

Decodable Words

Target Skill: Short *e*
Tess, step

Target Skill: Clusters with *s*
skip, spin, split, step, stick, still, stop

Previously Taught Skills
as, click, grin, has, Miss, tap, top, will

High-Frequency Words

New
was

Previously Taught
a, and, be, do, like, now, to

Who Likes to Jump?

page 98

Decodable Words
Target Skill: Short *u*
fun, Gus, jump, jumps, run, Russ, up

Target Skill: Final Clusters
and, bend, ends, fast, grasp, hands, jump, jumps, land, must, next, sand, went, wind

Previously Taught Skills
7, 8, 9, as, big, can, Fran, hill, his, hit, hop, is, it, Jill, legs, Len, Liz, on, track, will

High-Frequency Words
New
small, take

Previously Taught
a, her, like, likes, play, she, the, to, who, with

The Lost Cat

page 106

Decodable Words
Target Skill: Short *u*
hunt, Muff, must, us

Target Skill: Final Clusters
and, ask, desk, help, hint, hunt, last, lost, must, past, plant, rest, stand, task, Trent, went

Previously Taught Skills
at, Bess, can, cat, has, his, is, kits, Mick, not, plans, tracks, will, yes

High-Frequency Words
New
one, small, take

Previously Taught
find, her, here, I, said, see, the, to, we

The List

Decodable Words	**High-Frequency Words**
Target Skill: Short *u*	New
buns, but, hunts, nuts, run, runs	eat, put, take
Target Skill: Final Clusters	Previously Taught
and, best, Brent, fast, hunts, list, lost, mints, stamps, stand	a, he, I, said, the, this, too, what
Previously Taught Skills	
at, back, did, drops, eggs, get, gets, got, his, is, Mom, not, on, sack, snack, stop, tells	